10 Keys to Succeed in Business
A quick guide to Business Success

NYAMBE NAMANGOLWA WARREN

Copyright © 2018 NYAMBE NAMANGOLWA WARREN

All rights reserved.

ISBN-10:1719232741
ISBN-13:9781719232746

DEDICATION

This book is dedicated to my beloved wife Liywalii Angela and our two daughters Nakusheka and Sitali.

CONTENTS

Introduction 1

01. Change Your Altitude towards life 2

02. Take Some Risk 4

03. Seize Business Opportunities 6

04. Never give up 10

05. Use your time productively 12

06. Start small 18

07. Identify your talents 19

08. Be Honest 22

09. Think 23

10. Acknowledge God in all your ways 26

ACKNOWLEDGMENTS

I would to thank my wife Liywalii Angela for to her continued moral support during the time of writing this book. I would like also to thank Mr. Mushebe Millinger for the wonderful Business Discussions.

Introduction

Every person in this world wants to be successful. There is nothing wrong with that but the question is how can you succeed in business? What are the Keys to succeed in Business? This book answers these very important questions.

In this book you will discover the ten keys to succeed in Business. These ten Keys or ways are not only useful in the business world but in all areas of our life. These ten keys include among others the need to change our attitudes, take some reasonable risks, seizing the window of opportunities, the ability to think about our future and many more. The book also brings to you quotes from famous motivational speakers and authors.

It is my sincere hope that this book will be of help to you my dear reader.

01. Change Your Altitude towards life

"If you do not like something, change it. If you cannot change it, change your attitude." (Maya Angelou)

The first Key to business success is the need for you to change your attitude towards life. Change of attitude is vital if you are to be successful in life. Scholars state that, a positive attitude towards life is one of the personal characteristics of all successful people in the world. This chapter will define attitudes, types of attitudes and then how you can develop a positive attitude.

Michael defines altitudes as, 'internal beliefs that affect people how they see the world around them and he likens them to psychological filters that add meaning to every day events and communication'.

There are two types of attitudes and these are Positive and Negative attitudes. People who have a negative are less likely to be successful in life while people who are positive minded tend to be Successful.

So if you want to be successful stop harboring negative thought like, " I cannot make it in life because no one has ever been rich in our family or I cannot be rich because I am from a certain particular racial group." Self- reliance and being rich has nothing to do with your family background or the racial group you are coming from.

Here are three ways in which you can acquire positive attitudes:

Spend time with people who have positive attitudes.

These are people who are successful in life. Once you associate yourself with people who are have a positive altitudes you will also in the long run have positive attitudes towards life. Ben Carson in his *Book Think Big* points out clearly that it is vital to associate with the people you want to be like; if you want to be a doctor, associated yourself with doctors.

So the question that you should ask yourself is, what type of people do you associate with in your life? Are they positive or negative minded? Remember people say birds of the same feathers fly together.

02. Take Some Risk

"Risks may make you win, or they will make you learn. Either of the benefits is worth daring for." (Israelmore Ayivor)

The world we live in is full risks. The air we breathe in is risk because there are some air borne diseases that can affect us but you cannot say that I am not going to breathe in. boarding a plan is equally a risk because but the plans crash but you cannot say that I cannot travel using a plane. Everything you do in this world is risk but the worst that one can do is not to take risk.

Risk taking is very important because it brings a reward to your life. Let us take for example that you want to start a business which you think is going to be profitable and in turn improve your life from its current state. On the other hand there is a risk that your business will not be profitable; it will be total failure and many people are going to laugh at you. What are you going to do? Will go ahead with you planned business to realize the reward you have envisioned or not proceed with your plan and then remain the way you are? A reward is a motivating factor to the people who take risks. Our lord Jesus Christ also risked his life by leaving His Father's glorious Kingdom and came to this dark world to come redeem mankind because of the reward of redeeming man from sin.

Without risk taking we would still be taking many hours travelling, find it difficult to communicate with our beloved ones. The innovations that we have seen in the world have brought progress to human life but all these have come as result of risk taking.

People are afraid to take up some risks because they fear that they are going fail and people will laugh at them when they fail. In order for you to take up a risk you need first of all to evaluate the risk that you want to take. By this you have to look at the benefit that can be derived from it if all goes well. This should motivate you when you are taking a risk. I am not suggesting here that you should break the bank but take some risks that are in line with the law. What I mean is that you take some reasonable risk which does not require you to break the law.

03. Seize Business Opportunities

"Opportunities are like sunrises. If you wait too long, you miss them." *(William Arthur Ward)*

In the year 1995 Rob Glaser, after identifying a problem that the internet could not play both audio and video, he developed a software to play the audio and video on the internet. He founded the company RealNetworks; a company known worldwide. He turned what others considered a problem into a business opportunity. This success story shows the importance of seizing the window of opportunity.

Turn Problems to Opportunities.

The narrative above teaches us that, we should turn our problems into opportunities. Sometimes we fail to turn our problems into opportunities because we always on the complaining side. When you identify or face a problem, ask yourself, what can I do to solve this problem? Stop complaining but look for solutions because your complaint will not solve the problem.

What is an opportunity?

Barringer and Ireland defines an opportunity as, 'a favorable set of circumstances that creates a need for a new product, service or business'.

An opportunity should have the following four qualities:

- It should attractive.
- Durable.
- It should be timely.
- Finally it should be anchored in a product, service or business that creates or add value for its buyer or end user.

How can you identify business opportunities?

Opportunities are everywhere you set your eyes but the problem is that many people do not know how to identify opportunities. Here are ways in which you can identify opportunities:

Opportunity identification

- Observe the trends that are taking place in the economic, social, technological and political world and then identify a need that is not being satisfied and come up with a business that will solve the perceived need.
- You can also identify an opportunity by identify problems that people face in the world. This requires you to be on the listening side and not on the complaining side because it will be impossible to know the problem. Today there many big companies that have been formed in order to solve an identified problem.
- By identifying a gap in the market is actually another way in which you can come up with an opportunity that will in turn assist you to start a business. You can identify a gap in the market if you are observant. You scan the business environment and look at the businesses that are offering different products and services and identify their lapses and then provide a service or product to meet the gap you have identified. The can also be achieved by simply interviewing the clients who use the products or services whether these services or products are meeting their needs or not. Ask them the weakness have they have observed after using the services or products. You can also ask them to give some suggestions on how the products or

services should be provided if they are to meet their needs.

04. Never give up

"Stay strong, stay positive, and never give up." (Roy T. Bennett)

The world is full of famous people who never gave up in life despite facing some setbacks in their journey to success. One such story is that of Harland David Sanders also known Colonel Sanders the founder of Kentucky Fried Chicken (KFC) which is one of the well-known fast food companies in the world. At the age of 65 after retiring he used part of his social security check, equivalent to one hundred and five dollars, to start his business. He believed that restaurant owners would love his recipe; he went on knocking on their door to try to convince them to use his recipe for free at first but would get a percentage once the sale goes up. This was a very difficult task many people would have given up but Colonel pressed on. It is even reported that sometimes he would sleep in his car and dress a white suit in order for him to look formal.

When many people look at KFC they really nod their heads and think that this prosperity came by chance but they are not aware that the founder of the famous corporation received 1,009 rejections in his quest to persuade fast restaurants to use his recipe.

Dealing with rejection in Business

What do you do when clients reject your business ideas? What would you do when clients turn down your sales talk? Many times the answer is that many people give up. If you want to be successful you should emulate David Sanders who never gave up despite receiving 1,009 rejections.

You should believe in the business plan that you offering to the public. Once you believe in your plan, you will be able to press on and on trying to make it a reality. This will help you not to give up. This can be seen in the famous story of David Sanders. He believed in the business idea that he had. He believed that his business idea was good and was going to successful once implemented. This enabled him never to give up. If you do not believe in your business idea, who will believe in it?

If you are thinking of giving up now, my friend let me ask you, how many rejections have you received so far? Never give up in life!

05. Use your time productively
"Lost time is never found again." (Benjamin Franklin)

People say that time is money. What they actually mean is that time is very important. Hence you and I cannot be productive in life if we do not use our time productively. In this chapter we are going to look at how you can utilize your time productively. Every person today in the world you inclusive are given 24 hours a day and seven days a week in which you can achieve your goals. During this time that we are given, others achieve a great deal while others achieve less. The question is how do you spend your time so that that you reach your goals in life. Many people devote much of their day watching television programmes that are not, browsing the internet, gossiping others. This is not a good way of spending you time productively because these do not contribute to attaining your goals in life. Spending your time productively means that you will be able to reach you goals effectively and efficiently. One thing that you should bear in mind is that, time spend cannot be brought back.

If you use time productively you will achieve much in your life than someone who is misusing his or her time unproductively. Here are some proven principles that can assist you to effectively and efficiently utilize your time.

Set some goals in your life

Goal setting is an ingredient of being successful in business. So if you want to be successful your life you should need to set some goals in your life. You need to know your current financial status and then plan what you intent to achieve in the future. I have seen many people who are living their lives casually. The do not have goals in their lives. They are like a ride in the river which is being tossed to and fro by the water current of live.

Why it is important to set goals in life.

Goals are important in life because:

- Goals help you to be productive and have and have the sense of confidence in yourself.
- You will have targets to achieve in your life. As it has already been stated your goals should be specific, measurable, achievable, realistic and time bound.
- Goals help you to be focused in life.

Types of goals.

There are two types of goals; long term and short term goals. In order for you to successful in life you should have both short and long terms goals. Short term goals are goals which can be achieved within short period of time a period for example may be two years while long term goals are realized over a longer period of time for instance ten years or more.

How can you set goals in life?

Having identified the types of goals, let us now see how you can set some goals in your life. The first step is for you to get a pen and paper and then write down both your long and short term goals. It is very important to write down your goals because you will frequently be referring to this information each time you want to forget them. Your goals should be specific, measurable, achievable, and realistic and time bound.

Have a to-do list.

A have to do list is a tool that can help you to use your time productively. It is simply a list of activities to be accomplished and it shows the time when these activities are going to be achieved. It is recommended that these activities be written on a piece of paper or in a book.

Stop the bad habit of Procrastination

Procrastination is the number one hindrance to self-reliance in life. Many writers also have termed it as the thief of time. It has been defined as the postponement of important tasks to a later time or date. Procrastination is defined as putting off important tasks that are supposed to be accomplished for a later time. This reminds me of a story which is not true but teaches us a very important lesson of not procrastinating important tasks in life. This is the story of a bird which sings throughout the night when it the weather is cold. The song goes like this, 'tomorrow I will build a house, tomorrow I will build a house.' When the sun rises the bird forgets about the programme of constructing a house but again during the night when the weather is chilly it sings the same song.

You should have watch and a calendar.

All the activities that we plan to achieve in life will not come to fruition if we do not consider the time and day in which they can be accomplished.

Go to bed early and wake up early.

I have learnt a very important lesson from my experience of rearing chickens which I feel if applied in life can lead to enjoying good health and utilizing our time productively. Every day chickens wake up early and sleep early. Experts say that it is vital that we go to bed early sleep for eight hours. During this time the body will repair itself and it will be able to work at its optimum level the next day. Waking up early will help you to plan for the activities of the day and then stay focused during the day.

Experts advise that, adults needs about eight hours sleep. They also recommend that we go to sleep before midnight. Many people violet this important law because they go to bed late and sometimes they do not even sleep during the night. The body needs to rest so that it will be able to have the strength the next day's activities. God even saw the need for the body to rest when he gave the Sabbath. This is recorded in the Exodus 20: 8. He gave us to work for six days but to rest on the Seventh-Day because He Saw that man needed some rest.

Many diseases that many people suffer today in the world can directly related to not having abundant time to rest. I am not suggesting that you should spend all you time doing nothing because this leads to poverty.

So go to sleep early and woke up early and be productive during the time that you are awake.

06. Start small

'Big things have small beginnings' (Promethus)

Some people have failed to be successful in their careers or their businesses because they wanted to achieve bigger things in a short time. Everything in the world had its beginnings and mostly these have been smaller beginnings. Before you became an adult you were a baby. Before you completed your final grade you stated in the first grade. Others have gone even to say that, every journey begins with a step.

Most of the successful entrepreneurs in the world today started small. They saw their businesses growing from small businesses to big companies.

Do not be afraid to start small because todays' small Businesses will become the big corporations tomorrow.

07. Identify your talents

Use what talents you possess; the woods would be very silent if no birds sang there except those that sang best. (Henry van Dyke)

Every person in the world has a talent. The only problem is that we do not know how to identify them and utilize them for our own success in life. The Bible tells us the story of the three servants who were given some talent by their king to put into use so that when he came back from his long journey he would get some returns. The happy part of this story is that, two of the servant utilized their talents while the sad part is that one of the servants buried his talent or he did not use his talent. This chapter will in the first place define the term talent and then it will proceed to look at how you can identify your talents.

A talent is defined as a natural endowment of a person. In other words it the ability or natural capacity that we have, which ranges from our creativity to our athletic abilities.

Having defined the term talent, the question that you are asking now is, 'how can I identify my talent?' May I suggest to you five ways in which you can identify your talents. These ways are not conclusive but I feel they can assist you identify your talents. The following are the five ways in which you can identify your talents:

Listen to others

Listening to what others tell us is the first direction to help us identify our talents. The problem with many of us is that we are not good listeners. Many people have been telling you that you are good at something but you have not listened and then sit down and then develop that for your benefit. I agree with Daniel Chunga when he says that, "God has given us two ears to listen more and speak less."

Identify what you find easy doing.

The thing that you find easy doing could be your talent. When others find it very difficult doing these things with you is a walk over.

Do what you enjoy most.

You should ask yourself, 'what are the things that I enjoy doing most in life?'. These could be your talents. It is important to identify what you enjoy doing most in life and then turn them into your talent because this enjoyment will act as the driving force as you keep on going in life and you will not easily give up due to the fact that you are enjoying what you are doing.

Ask people.

Asking people to assist us identify our talents is very important also. You should ask people who know you well to tell you what they think you are good at. During this process ask them to ignore your weak points or your bad habit and concentrate on you positive side. This can be done one to one.

Asking people to assist with talent identification is very important because, these people know us better than we know ourselves. They know our deeds both good and bad because they are the recipients of our deeds.

08. Be Honest

"Whoever is careless with the truth in small matters cannot be trusted with important matters." (Albert Einstein)

Being honest is a recipe for being successful in business. When you are honest you clients will be willing to do business with you. On the contrary when you are not honest you do not follow business ethics.

Many successful people or businesses use dubious means in order to achieve their goals. Others even use substances which are harmful the human body. They keep their dishonest deeds secret and present a good public image to the world. What they are forgetting is that God is watching the evil works.

When you are honest you will also learn to appreciate that whatever you have comes from God and you will be able to return a faithful tithe to God's work. The word of God in the Book of Malachi 3: 9 says, 'will a man rob God?' Yet you rob me but you ask, 'how do we rob you?' the lord continued, 'in tithe and offerings.' God is asking us to be honest even in the way we manage our businesses.

09. Think

'If you think you can, you can. And if you think you cannot, you are right' (Mary Kay Ash)

There are many young and old men and women today in the world who do not take time to think about their present and future state of lives. Mary kay said it correctly that, success or failure has to do with what you educate your brain. Mark Finley in his book Satisfied says that, 'if you tell yourself long enough that you are a loser, you will lose. If you repeat it often enough no matter how untrue, it will become reality to you.' The Holy Scriptures also states that, 'as a man thinks so is he.' Commenting on the true work of education, my favorite writer Ellen White states that true education should, "train the youths to be thinkers, and not mere reflectors of other men's thought." This famous quotes show the importance attached to thinking. Ask yourself whether you do take time to think about your life.

God has given us the brain to think about our lives; what we can achieve in this life with the time God has granted us. Experts say that people use a smaller percentage of their brain. Many people are distracted from taking time think by the media. They spent most of their precious time watching movies and Television. Considering the fact that most of the movies take long to watch; others even go up to three hours. Bearing this in mind it is seen that it will be very difficult for one to find time think. However you should find time think about your life. All the famous successful people in the world find time to think. Bill gate for instance says that every year he travels to place where he cannot disturbed and spends time thinking about his the future of his company Microsoft.

One thing that I have discovered is that distractions hinder many people from thinking critically. These distractions can come from our friends, family members or the media. Because of this we fail to concentrate on what we are thinking about. To solve this predicament you should find time when you are free from disturbances. This could be early in the morning when everyone is asleep or during the night when everyone has gone to bed. During this time when there are no distractions, take time to concentrate on your work. If you do not find time for you to concentrate on your work you will end up assisting other people to achieve their goals in life.

When you are thinking about your life you should think about where you are now, where you want to be and what steps you should take to arrive where you want to be. Commenting on the importance of thinking Daniel Chunga in his book *How to be Self-Reliant* had it right when he said that, 'if you cannot think you will sink'. What he meant was that it that, if you do not take time to think about your future, you cannot have one. You will be busy blaming others for your adversities. These blames will only exacerbate the problem and not solve the problem. In our culture there is a saying which says that, 'a lazy person will always blame his or her tools.' As a result you will be used by others to fulfill their goals

10. Acknowledge God in all your ways

Trust in the LORD with all your heart; lean not on your understanding. In all your ways acknowledge him, and He shall direct your path. (Proverbs 3: 5- 6)

In everything that you achieve or do not forget that you are a creature and not God. So you should acknowledge God.

A story is told in the Bible of the Rich fool who had a bumper harvest in a particular year so much so that he had nowhere to store his crops. This he said, "I will do, I will pull down my bun and erect big ones and then after that I will tell enjoy what you have laid up all these years." But when god realized that the rich fool was self- centered because he did not acknowledge as the giver of everything he had and that he did not want to share with the poor, the lord said that he would take his spirit from and then see who is going to eat whatever he has worked for.

The same message still applies to you and me. It is the lord who is protecting your life every day and night and we should give him the glory and honor. When you embark on the journey of being successful you should first of all pray and seek for guidance from God in all your plans.

Learn also to share what you have with the less privileged. There are many poor people in the world today. Some of these poor people did not chose to be poor but may be it is due circumstances. May be others are chronically sick and they are crippled. We should learn to share what we have with the poor.

www.ingramcontent.com/pod-product-compliance
Lightning Source LLC
Chambersburg PA
CBHW030043230526
45472CB00005B/1650